{ *Little-Known* FACTS ABOUT *Well-Known* PLACES }

PARIS

Little-Known FACTS ABOUT Well-Known PLACES

PARIS

DAVID HOFFMAN

METRO BOOKS
NEW YORK

Images: Jupiterimages.com

Metro Books
122 Fifth Avenue
New York, NY 10011

ISBN-13: 978-1-4351-0427-3

Printed and bound in the United States of America

1 3 5 7 9 10 8 6 4 2

INTRODUCTION

Italy, Paris, New York...just hear their names and dozens of familiar images come to mind. But for everything that we may know about these (and other) favorite places, there is always a tidbit, a top secret, or a twist of fate that we have yet to discover.

Little-Known Facts about Well-Known Places goes beyond the obvious to reveal the stories behind the stories regarding the cities, countries, and tourist destinations that we all are familiar with—or at least think we're familiar with.

Covering every aspect—from food, film, and fashion to people, history, art, and architecture—these collections of offbeat facts and figures, statistics and specifics, are guaranteed to delight a first-time visitor and surprise even the most jaded local.

Packed with a wealth of revelations that could start (or stop) a conversation—not to mention win a ton of bar bets—*Little-Known Facts about Well-Known Places* is a must-have for know-it-alls, information addicts, curious readers, armchair travelers, and pop culture junkies of all ages.

Look for these other
titles in the series

Little-Known
FACTS
ABOUT
Well-Known
PLACES

ITALY

NEW YORK

DISNEYLAND

IRELAND

Paris is the "City of Light," yet the nickname has nothing to do with the wattage put out by the 276 monuments, hotels, churches, fountains, bridges, and canals that illuminate the city every evening. Instead, the "light" of Paris refers to the intellectuals, artists, writers, and musicians who made it the cultural center of the world in the 1920s. Not that the bulbs don't help...

Photographs of the Eiffel Tower have long been public domain, but in 2003, the company that runs the landmark purposely installed and copyrighted a new lighting display on the structure, so that all nighttime images of the lit tower taken after that date could not be commercially printed or published without permission—or, more importantly, a fee.
[Profits help maintain the tower.]

20,000

bulbs currently illuminating the
Eiffel Tower

42 MILES

distance visible, on a clear day and
in every direction, from the top of
the Eiffel Tower

200 MILLION

visitors to the Eiffel Tower
since its opening

300

design proposals Gustave Eiffel beat
out for the contract to build
"an opening archway" to the
1889 Paris World's Fair

The Paris World's Fair committee called Gustave Eiffel's Tower design a "beautiful, transparent, structure" and selected it because it utilized novel techniques in architecture—and because it was the least expensive submission to build.

The city's original intention was to knock down the Eiffel Tower after 20 years and sell it for scrap. All that changed when Gustave Eiffel, realizing that his structure would survive if he could find a practical use for it, persuaded the military to lease it as a base for a long-range radio tower.

While the Eiffel Tower had always been designed with space to house shops and restaurants on the first and second levels, Gustave Eiffel had sole usage of the room at the top. According to historians, it served as a trysting place—and, no surprise—he discovered that being able to bring dates up several elevators to the highest spot in Paris was the ultimate chick magnet.

The Eiffel Tower is the most popular paid-admission tourist attraction in the world.

The Eiffel Tower isn't made of steel, but of puddle iron—a type of wrought iron with a higher tensile strength.

In 1925, the Eiffel Tower was in need of refurbishing and there was talk of tearing it down rather than repairing it. Seeing an opportunity, con man Victor Lustig convinced a scrap iron dealer that he was authorized to sell the landmark on the city's behalf. Once he had swindled the money from his mark, Lustig fled to Austria. However, when he discovered that his victim had been too embarrassed to report the incident, he brazenly headed back to Paris, contacted another scrap dealer...and sold the tower a second time.

The Eiffel Tower—which stands at 1,063 feet—has spawned twenty architectural replicas around the world, ranging in height from 10 feet (in front of a construction company in Kazakhstan) to 540 feet (outside the Paris Hotel in Las Vegas).

In order to give it an even greater illusion of height, the Eiffel Tower is painted in three shades of a color (which can vary; right now, it's brown), with the lightest shade at the top and the darkest at the bottom.

50 TONS
amount of paint it
takes to paint the
Eiffel Tower

19
times, since construction,
that the tower has been
painted; the most recent
paint job began in 2008

15 MONTHS
time it takes to paint
the tower, from start
to finish

7 YEARS
standard interval
between paintings of
the tower

The fastest way to enter the Eiffel Tower (and avoid waiting in any line) is to make a reservation at the Jules Verne restaurant on the second floor of the Eiffel Tower. It has a private entrance and elevator reserved exclusively for patrons. All this privilege has a price: With renowned chef Alain Ducasse now installed at the helm of the restaurant, the price of lunch averages $108 a person.

When the Jules Verne restaurant underwent remodeling in 2007, it was vital that the new design do nothing to strain the then 119-year-old structure, so anything that was torn down or taken out was weighed, as was every piece that was moved back in to replace it. As part of the renovation, the restaurant's windows were fitted with special glass that allows diners to enjoy the spectacular view at night, even when all the lights are on in the room.

In the 1600s, Clément Lassagne, personal chef to French aristocrat Marshal César duc de Choiseul, comte du Plessis-Praslin, developed a sugar-coated almond confection in his employer's honor. Lassagne's "Praslines" became so popular that when the French colonized Louisiana, the candy went with them. There, the recipe was tweaked—something had to be done with all the pecans in the area—and thanks to the local dialect, the name as well as the spelling changed from prasline to praline.

In 1889, hotelier Stephanie Tatin was making an apple tart for guests when, distracted, she inadvertently put the cooked apples in a pie tin before she had lined it with piecrust. Oops. Thinking quickly, she placed the pastry dough on top of the apples, baked the whole thing, and inverted it onto a plate when it was done. Everyone loved it, word of the dessert spread—and soon her Tarte Tatin was featured on menus all over Paris.

Paris Brest is a popular round pastry filled with a praline butter cream and topped with toasted almonds. The name comes from the cycling tournament that once ran from Paris to Brest to Paris. Pastry chef Louis Durand, who had a shop along the route, created this circular variation on the éclair, designed to resemble a bicycle wheel.

Since pastry is a luxury, it follows that the better the neighborhood in Paris, the better the cakes. Hence, a window full of meringues is the unmistakable sign of a pedestrian pastry shop.

Dark-edged fruit in a tart
indicates canned fruit; fresh fruit
caramelizes evenly.

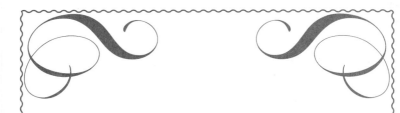

Bread baked in big round loaves stays fresh a lot longer than bread baked in long, thin loaves.

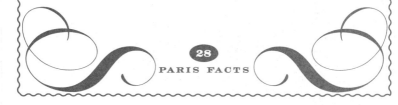

Although synonymous
with France, the croissant
originated in Budapest in
1686, and did not become a
staple of Parisian bakeries
until well into the
twentieth century.

Up until the mid-1700s, *restaurant* was the French term for a restorative broth prepared for those not able to digest solid foods. When a soup vendor named Boulanger opened a food service business in Paris in 1765, the sign above his door announced "restaurants"—and eventually, the word came to mean *where* you ate, instead of *what* you ate.

CARTE du JOUR

The French Revolution spawned the restaurant revolution: Prior to 1789, chefs worked exclusively in the homes of the wealthy; ordinary people prepared their own meals. After the Revolution, many chefs found themselves out of work, so they took to the idea of feeding the masses in a public setting, at a set price for a set meal.

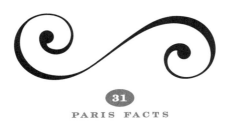

By the Numbers

12,452
restaurants and cafés in Paris

136
tea salons in Paris

392
glasses of wine the average French person drinks per year (down from 676 glasses in the 1960s)

500
snails the average French person eats per year

The term *bistro*—used to describe a small, neighborhood, family-run French restaurant—most likely derives from the Russian word *bystro*, meaning "quickly." It dates back to the Russian occupation of Paris around 1814, when Cossack soldiers, thinking that the workers at a café were too slow, would rudely shout out "Bystro! Bystro!" in hopes of speeding up the service.

In 1900, as a way to promote their family's tire business, Andre and Edouard Michelin compiled a list of road trip-related services (gas stations, public toilets, food, and lodging), which they gave to garages to give to their clients for free. When they learned that one Paris garage was using their allotment to prop up a broken bench, the Michelins knew they needed to guarantee that their guide would be taken seriously, so they began to not just list restaurant names, but to review them...and the world-famous Michelin Guides were born!

By the Numbers

390
Paris restaurants the Michelin Guide
currently visits and reviews

18 MONTHS
frequency, according to
Michelin, that each establishment
is visited and reviewed

3.5 YEARS
frequency, according to a
former employee, that many
establishments are actually visited
and reviewed

10
Paris restaurants with coveted
3-star Michelin rating

o attract publicity for his Montmartre supper club in the 1920s, Joe Zelli decided to adorn the place with caricatures of the celebrities that frequented his establishment. He hired a twenty-year-old American studying painting in France, whose sketches proved so popular that they not only covered the walls, they forever changed the career path of the young artist—Al Hirschfeld—responsible for them.

During the two weeks leading up to Christmas, Berthillon—the landmark ice cream shop in the Ile St. Louis—is so popular and so crowded that a police officer is assigned to the area simply to direct the flow of Parisians queuing up for glaces and sorbets.

For a few days in October, the climbing vine covering the rue Blanche Fire Station in the 9th arrondissement yields a grape harvest, from which a non-alcoholic wine is made, bottled, and sold under the Chateau Blanche label. The cuvée is named for the department chief that year.

In 1863, from his lab in Neuilly-sur-Seine, chemist Angelo Mariani concocted a beverage combining red Bordeaux wine with coca leaves. His Vin Mariani cocawine was an international success and inspired George Pemberton, a Columbus, Georgia, pharmacist, to develop a non-alcoholic version. Instead of using wine, Pemberton mixed coca leaves with syrup made from kola nuts and called his beverage Coca-Cola.

Movie star Gérard Depardieu owns about a dozen vineyards around the world, has his own wine label, and takes his passion for the grape so seriously that his passport identifies him as *acteur-vigneron*—or actor-winemaker.

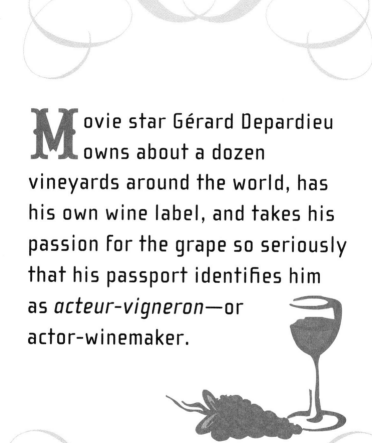

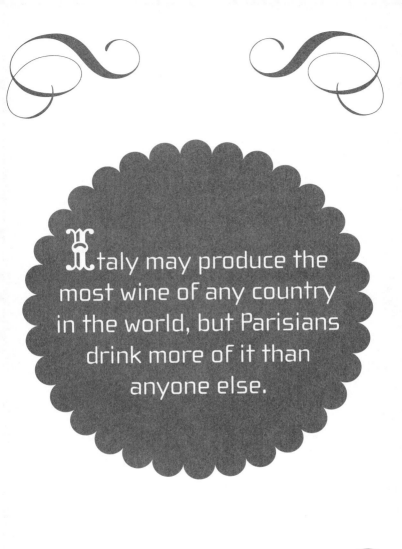

Italy may produce the most wine of any country in the world, but Parisians drink more of it than anyone else.

When the French count using their fingers, they start with the thumb. That means holding up an index finger to order a glass of wine (or cup of coffee) in Paris is likely to get you two; the thumb will be counted, even if it is curled out of sight.

Louis XVI believed that not drinking wine was a sign of fanaticism and blamed the barbarity of the French Revolution on the fact that its leader, Robespierre, drank only water.

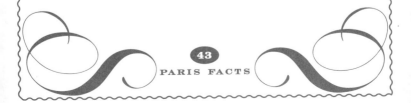

Louis Pasteur developed the process of pasteurization in the 1850s as a way to prevent wine spoilage. Only after did he realize that it could also be used to preserve milk.

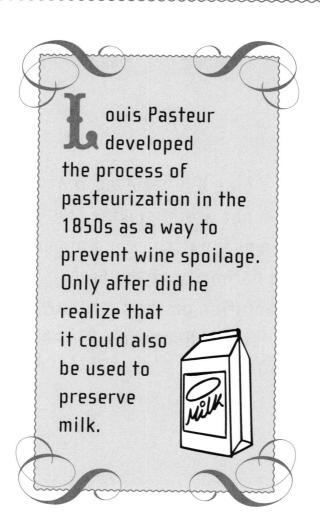

Dom Perignon was a master winemaker and he definitely perfected champagne, but the Benedictine monk did not, as commonly reported, create it or invent it accidentally. The legend of Dom Perignon was invented by Dom Groussard, one of Dom Perignon's successors at the abbey of Hautvillers, who concoted the tale in order to increase the profile of his church and to bring it historical significance.

When religious rules prevented them from eating meat, monks in eighteenth-century Europe frequently turned to cheese as a primary source of protein—and soon began to produce their own. As a result, many well-known varieties of French cheeses, such as Port Salut, Maroilles, Livarot, Pont-l'Eveque, and Saint-Nectaire, bear the names of the monasteries where they were first made.

By the Numbers

500
approximate number of cheeses
produced in France

45 POUNDS
amount of cheese consumed in
France, per person, annually

30 MONTHS
ideal aging time to bring Comté
cheese to its full flavor

$50
price per pound of the highly
coveted, available only in-season
Brillat-Savarin aux Truffles

Napoleon did not invent Napoleon pastry or Neapolitan ice cream, nor was either dessert named in his honor. Rather, both dishes came to Paris from southern Italy, and their names derive from *napolitain*, the French adjective for the city of Naples.

Perhaps it was a need to figure out how to keep track of all the land he had conquered that prompted Napoleon to formulate the modern system of street address numbering, which places even numbers on the south and east sides, and odd numbers on the north and west.

By the Numbers

720,000 SQUARE MILES
total land that Napoleon conquered

5' 2"
Napoleon's height

17,000
beheadings during the French Revolution

On their wedding night, Napoleon was bitten on the leg by Josephine's pug, Fortune, who mistook their throes of passion for an attack on his owner. It was this injury—and the fact that Josephine spent the evening putting compresses on her husband's wound—that (incorrectly) led to the oft-told story that the two never consummated their marriage.

Containing some 250 species, the Empress Josephine's rose garden at Malmaison Chateau was so revered worldwide, that during the French Revolution—even though all official trade with England had ceased—officials for both countries permitted a top British nurseryman to go behind French battle lines to deliver a new variety (Hume's Blush Tea-scented China) and to care for her flowers.

After his victory over Russia and Austria at Austerlitz in 1805, Napoleon promised his troops that he would take them back to France, where they would "pass under arches of triumph" on their way to their homes. He kept his word; construction of the Arc de Triomphe began the following year.

By the Numbers

31 YEARS

length of time to complete the
Arc de Triomphe

164 FEET

height of the Arc de Triomphe

148 FEET

width of the Arc de Triomphe

72 FEET

thickness of the Arc de Triomphe

128

names of Napoleonic battle victories
inscribed on the white walls under
the vault of the Arc de Triomphe

Napoleon's original plan to honor his army's victory at the Battle of Austerlitz was not quite as tasteful (or as literal) as a triumphal arch. Early designs, and even a scale model that was built and briefly displayed at the Place de la Bastille, envisioned a 160-foot-high elephant cast in bronze from melted down cannons seized in his military conquests. The elephant squirted water from its trunk.

You would think that the Arc de Triomphe would have been enough, yet the design of La Madeleine, a church in the 8th arrondissement of Paris, was also commissioned in 1806 and pays homage to Napoleon. Fifty-two columns surround the perimeter of the building—one for each year of the emperor's life.

The art nouveau public toilets, located just outside La Madeleine, are not only spectacular (and practical!); they have officially been declared a historical monument.

The term ART NOUVEAU

is derived from Siegfried Bing's Paris gallery, Maison de l'Art Nouveau, which, when it opened in 1895, was the first venue to showcase new works—pottery, glass, textiles, jewelry, silver, and furniture, as well as paintings—characterized by highly stylized linear curves and floral or plant-inspired motifs.

In 1966, the artist Salvador Dali created the sundial that adorns the wall of the building at 27 rue Saint-Jacques in the 5th arrondissement—a gift for friends who owned a shop nearby. The face of the sundial resembles a woman's face, but its shape is that of a scallop shell—a reference to coquille Saint-Jacques, the famous French scallop dish, and to the street's name.

The black granite sphere on a white marble base in the center of the main courtyard of the Palais Bourbon is a sculpture by American artist Walter de Maria—who, in the mid-1960s, was the drummer for the rock group Velvet Underground.

The "thinker" depicted in the famous Rodin statue is the poet Dante.

Although he was introduced to art at a young age and later collected Impressionist works, Paul Gauguin spent eleven years as a Paris stockbroker—and even labored for a year as a worker on the Panama Canal—before he decided to pursue painting.

The Y-shaped UNESCO headquarters is home to both a swarm of diplomats and an amazing modern art collection (more than 500 pieces), including the largest Picasso ever painted. *The Fall of Icarus* is composed of forty wooden panels and measures approximately 30' x 35' (covering just under 1,000 square feet).

The most attended exhibition mounted to date at the modern art museum inside the Centre Georges Pompidou was the 2007 retrospective devoted to artist Hergé, the creator of the comic book character, Tintin.

Built in the 1970s, the Centre Georges Pompidou appears to be constructed inside-out, with its structural framework and ductwork visible on the exterior. The ducts are color-coded by function: Blue ducts carry air, green ducts carry liquids, yellow signifies electrical systems, and red is for elevators—"movement and flow"—and for fire prevention systems.

Constantin Brancusi moved to Paris from his native Romania in 1903, and pioneered abstract modernist sculpture. His most famous work, *The Kiss*—carved of limestone and regarded as perhaps the quintessential representation of love in twentieth-century art—is not found in one of the city's top museums, however, but in the Montparnasse Cemetery.

After health concerns discouraged burials within the city limits, Napoleon established Père-Lachaise Cemetery outside Paris in 1804. The distant location, however, made many reluctant to buy plots, so the emperor had the remains of celebrated French folks—Molière, La Fontaine, and star-crossed lovers Pierre Abélard and Héloïse—dug up and moved to the newly established resting place. He theorized that the public, eager to be buried among the famous, would follow. He was right; today the "residents" at Père-Lachaise number over 300,000.

ère-Lachaise Cemetery is the most visited cemetery in the world and while Colette, Chopin, Edith Piaf, Marcel Proust, Maria Callas, and Oscar Wilde (just to name a few) are all interred there, the most visited graveside—attracting 1,000 people daily—belongs to Jim Morrison. That is assuming he is indeed buried there. On seeing the grave, Doors' drummer John Densmore deduced it was "too short," starting the rumor that the site was actually empty or held the remains of someone else.

French playboy and journalist Victor Noir was killed in a duel for having ridiculed a relative of Napoleon III, and the life-size bronze figure that adorns his burial site at Père-Lachaise depicts him lying flat on his back, exactly as he was when he fell to his death. The statue has obtained cult status, thanks primarily to the sizeable bulge in Noir's pants—and the legend that rubbing that area (which has been polished to a shine from being touched so frequently) will increase fertility and bring luck in love.

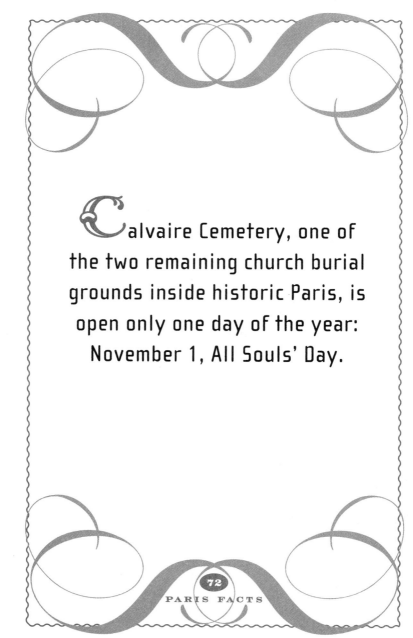

Calvaire Cemetery, one of the two remaining church burial grounds inside historic Paris, is open only one day of the year: November 1, All Souls' Day.

The concrete slabs with the interesting Gothic inscriptions found in the courtyard at 26 rue Chanoinesse, a quaint cobblestone street near the cathedral of Notre-Dame, are tombstones from a religious establishment that was once located on the Ile de la Cité.

The cathedral of Notre-Dame offers confession in French, English, Spanish, Italian, German, Portuguese, Arabic, and Japanese.

Because Notre-Dame was built in a time of illiteracy, the frescoes, stained-glass windows, and statuary are not only decorative, but were designed to tell the story of the Bible, in chronological order.

While the myriad carved stone figures that adorn Notre-Dame are commonly referred to as gargoyles, most should properly be called architectural grotesques. The term "gargoyle" refers specifically to a grotesque with a spout that collects rainwater and directs it away from the building. Grotesques that serve a purely ornamental or artistic function—and there are many at Notre-Dame—are called *chimeras*.

The name "gargoyle" originated from the French gargouille, meaning "throat" or "gullet."

By the Numbers

225

steps from the north tower at
Notre-Dame up to the stony bestiary
of gargoyles, gremlins, and demons

180 YEARS

time it took to build Notre-Dame

3,000

capacity of Notre-Dame,
with 1,400 seated

13 MILLION

people who annually visit Notre-Dame,
making it most popular tourist site
in Paris

Point Zero is the official name of the circular marker situated in the square in front of Notre-Dame. It is from here that the distance from Paris to every city and town in France and vice versa is measured.

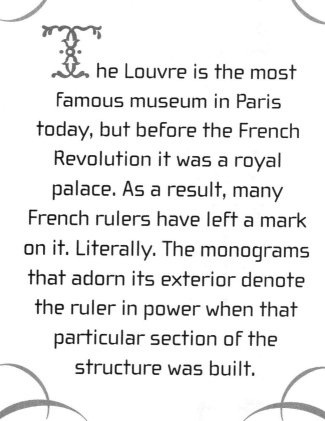

The Louvre is the most famous museum in Paris today, but before the French Revolution it was a royal palace. As a result, many French rulers have left a mark on it. Literally. The monograms that adorn its exterior denote the ruler in power when that particular section of the structure was built.

Although not scientifically proven, art historians have theorized that the unique glaze used by Martin Drolling in his 1815 painting, *L'intérieur d'une cuisine*, which hangs in the Sully wing at the Louvre, is a mix of oil and *mumie*—the organic substance that is secreted from a ground up human heart.

By the Numbers

380,000
works of art in the Louvre inventory

35,000
works of art on display in the Louvre at any given time

52
works by Rubens in the Louvre

12
works by Rembrandt in the Louvre

249
works by Leonardo da Vinci in the Louvre
(more than in Italy, or anyplace else)

I.M. Pei's spectacular glass pyramid in the front courtyard of the Louvre is not to be missed, but it is not the best place to enter the museum, due to the interminable lines. Better to head in through the Passage Richelieu, the Galerie du Carrousel, or (particularly for first-time visitors), the Porte des Lions, as that doorway puts you closest to *Mona Lisa*.

Mona Lisa may now be the most famous painting in the world, but when it remained unfinished after four years, Francesco del Giocondo, the man who commissioned it, refused it. Leonardo da Vinci eventually sold it to King Francis I of France on the condition that the king (and eventually the Louvre) could not take immediate possession. Until the day he died, Leonardo kept the painting hanging on a wall of his home.

$105,000
original selling price of *Mona Lisa*
(in current dollars)

$670,000,000
current estimated insured value
of *Mona Lisa*

$0
cost to see *Mona Lisa*, if you go to
the Louvre on the first Sunday of the
month or on Bastille Day, July 14

7.5 MILLION
current estimate of the number of
people who view *Mona Lisa* at the
Louvre each year

Attendance at the Louvre rose from an average of 6 million in 2000 to 7.5 million in 2005. Museum officials are mum on the matter, but most in the art world call this the "*The Da Vinci Code* Effect"—attributing the visitor increase and interest to the more than 61 million copies (in 44 languages) that have been sold of Dan Brown's novel.

So as not to block the view of the Louvre during the day, but in order to efficiently illuminate the bridge at night, the art deco street lamps along the Pont du Carrousel incorporated a telescoping mechanism (no longer in use), whereby they could be raised from a height of 12 meters to 22 meters whenever they were lit.

Pont de la Concorde was built in 1792 and is made of stone from the demolished Bastille, so people will "forever tramp the ancient fortress underfoot" every time they cross the bridge.

The Bastille may have housed prisoners, but at least it did it with style: Inmates had their own furniture and servants, and the accommodations were more like apartments than cells.

France's national day, July 14, was not officially intended to mark the 1789 storming of the Bastille. While it is known as Bastille Day in English, the holiday's proper name is the Fête de la Fédération, and it celebrates the institution of France's constitutional monarchy, which was officially inaugurated on July 14, 1790—one year after the fall of the Bastille.

The iconic French tricolor flag was proposed by General Lafayette—the same Lafayette who served alongside George Washington in the American Revolutionary War—in the months following the fall of the Bastille. The flag's three, equal-sized vertical stripes—in white, red, and blue—symbolized an equal union of the monarchy (white was the color of the ruling Bourbon family) and the people (red and blue being the official colors of Paris).

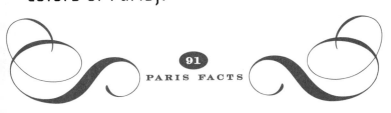

In all probability, the expression *frog*, used as a slang (some say derogatory) term for the French, owes its origins to the French flag, which originally had a blue background with a gold fleur-de-lys on it. The English, not knowing that the fleur-de-lys was a stylized design of a flower, mistakenly perceived it to be a frog.

For centuries, the French celebrated New Year's Day on April 1, and when France adopted the Gregorian calendar in 1564, many residents forgot to make the switch. In Paris, it became common to mock the clueless by playing tricks on them; anyone who fell for these pranks was dubbed a *poisson d'Avril* (an April Fish)—or an April Fool.

The 400-foot lighthouse that marks the location of La Criée du Phare fish market might look like it has stood guard over Paris for several centuries, but it has only been in the city since 1966, when it was towed in from Brittany.

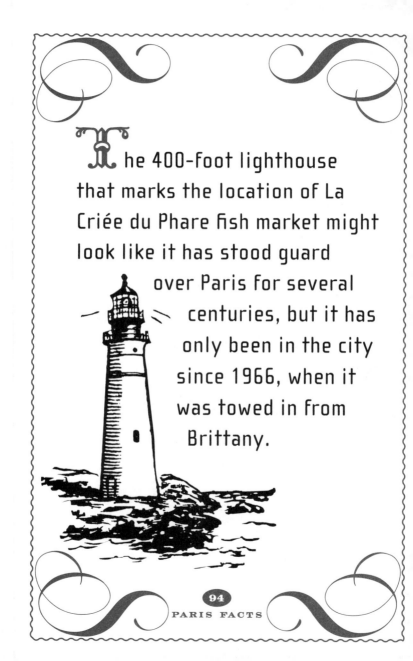

The Marché des Enfants Rouge,
a covered food market in the
3rd arrondissement, is one of the
oldest in Paris. It was scheduled
to be demolished in 1994, but the
building underwent a six-year
renovation instead. Some speculate
that officials opted to save it after
remembering that a psychic had
predicted that the neighboring houses
would collapse should the market ever
be destroyed. Paris is, after all, home
to more than 6,000 astrologers.

Most companies in Paris receive job applications via e-mail or online, yet many also ask that prospective employees submit a handwritten letter. This is so they have a handwriting sample that can be reviewed by graphologists, who analyze the handwriting to determine whether the applicant is right for the position.

Paul Chasse, a garage mechanic in the Kremlin-Bicetre area of Paris, turned his talent for tinkering toward toys in 1958, when he rigged up an automatic drawing device that didn't need batteries and had no loose parts. His *L'Ecran Magique* (Magic Screen) generated interest when first demonstrated in Germany, and it reached international acclaim in 1960, when the American company Ohio Art, began to market it under the name Etch A Sketch.

Eight million traffic tickets are issued in Paris every year; 7.5 million of those are for illegal parking.

In Paris it is not uncommon to see drivers bumping the cars in front and back of them as they maneuver in and out of parking spaces. Probably the best explanation for this: A French driver's license, while hard to get, is good for life. Once a person has one, they never have to renew it or take the written or road tests again—regardless of age, mental competence, or physical condition.

French law states that driver's license photos—or any photos for government-issued IDs—cannot be taken with the subject wearing any form of headwear, even if it is for religious reasons.

In 1881, before newspaper photography was widely used, journalist Arthur Meyer opened a wax museum in Paris filled with replicas of newsmakers, so the public could see the "faces" of the famous folks they had only read about in the papers. The museum is now known as the Musée Grevin.

The collection at the Musée Grevin includes 500 figures, most with ties to France, from Voltaire to Charles de Gaulle to Ernest Hemingway. Three hundred are on display at any given time; the one with whom visitors have their picture taken most frequently is the life-size reproduction of Barbie.

If the mineral gypsum is heated to 150°C, it produces a form of calcium sulfate—the key component to dry plaster. The abundance of gypsum in the subsoil of Paris' Montmartre district was crucial to building the great structures of Europe. When this plaster was exported to the United States, it became known as Plaster of Paris.

The French gave the Statue of Liberty to the United States, but they kept one—actually more than one—for themselves. There are three Statues of Liberty in Paris alone. One replica sits in the Luxembourg Gardens; a second, a 1:16 scale model from which the original was fabricated, is in the Musée des Arts et Métiers; and the third stands on Swan Island in the Seine. The last was a gift to France from the community of Americans living in Paris in 1889.

The bronze equestrian statue of French king Henry IV at the center of the Pont-Neuf is actually a replica. The original, erected in 1618 by the king's wife, was melted down in 1792, to make cannons during the French Revolution; the replacement, somewhat fittingly made by melting two statues of Napoleon and using the original cast, was installed in 1818.

The Molière Fountain at 3 rue Richelieu, built in 1841, was the first statue in Paris to honor someone other than a king.

The statue at the entrance of the Comédie Française (The National Theater of France) is of French actor François Joseph Talma, a favorite of Napoleon's. Talma was among the artists who spearheaded the use of scenery and costumes, and at a time when actors wore their own clothes while performing (regardless of whether they suited the role), he revolutionized live theater with his decision to appear on stage in Voltaire's *Brutus* wearing a toga.

espite Shakespeare's popularity with Paris theater-goers, the Bard's *Henry V*—in which the English defeat of the French at the Battle of Agincourt figures prominently—was not performed in the city until 1999.

Other than a prominent nose, the real Cyrano de Bergerac had little in common with the hero of the nineteenth-century Edmond Rostand play bearing his name; in fact, historians speculate that the real Cyrano was gay, and the model for Roxanne was his cousin.

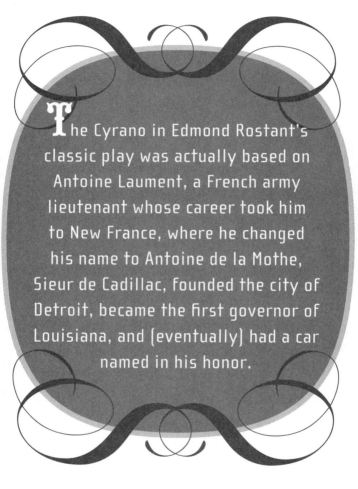

The Cyrano in Edmond Rostant's classic play was actually based on Antoine Laument, a French army lieutenant whose career took him to New France, where he changed his name to Antoine de la Mothe, Sieur de Cadillac, founded the city of Detroit, became the first governor of Louisiana, and (eventually) had a car named in his honor.

At the age of seventeen, before he became famous for writing the comic plays on which the operas *The Barber of Seville* and *The Marriage of Figaro* were based, Pierre de Beaumarchais pioneered the development of the modern wristwatch, by inventing a mechanism that made time pieces more accurate and compact. So revolutionary was his compact, accurate design that Jean-Andre Lepaute, Royal Clockmaker to King Louis XV, tried to pass off the teenager's innovation as his own.

Many of the streets in the area surrounding the Palais Garnier (the Paris Opera House)—Auber, Meyerbeer, Halevy, Scribe, and Gluck—got their names from noted nineteenth-century opera composers and librettists.

The selection of Carlos Ott, a young Canadian architect, to design the Bastille Opera House, might have been an error—at least according to many in the know, who claim that former French president François Mitterand was briefed to pick, out of five models on display in a blind competition, "the one on the far left," a design by Richard A. Meier. But Mitterand misunderstood his aides' instructions and, by mistake, chose the one on the far right—which was Ott's.

A trapeze artist, who also inspired the 1867 song, "The Daring Young Man on the Flying Trapeze," wowed French audiences with his ability to turn somersaults in mid-air. In need of something specific to wear while performing, he came up with a skin-tight one-piece garment that covered the torso, but left the legs free. His design, which allowed unrestricted movement, caught on with the ballet studios of Paris, and the circus costume-turned-dancewear took its name from its inventor, Jules Leotard.

A high-kicking "happy dance" that French schoolgirls did to celebrate the end of exams made its way into the Paris music halls, where it evolved and was performed chorus-line style. The routine revealed the dancers' petticoats, which resembled a duck's tail feathers. The French word for duck—*canard*—was abbreviated to give the dance its name: the Can Can.

In the gallery at the Conservatoire National des Arts et Métiers that exhibits the collection of laboratory instruments used by French scientist Antoine-Laurent Lavoisier, the acoustics are such that two people—standing on opposite sides of the room, facing the walls, and with their backs to each other—can easily have a conversation, without anyone in the center of the room hearing a word. At one time the room was used by monks to hear confession from those with contagious diseases.

A prominent Paris physician concerned about the heartless nature of execution by axe (it could take as many as six chops before the head was severed) developed a machine to do the job more humanely. Yet, while the suggested beheading machine did its job well, to his dismay, Joseph Guillotin's name became forever linked to execution by guillotine.

Contrary to common lore, Joseph Guillotin was not killed by the machine that bears his name; he died at home, in bed, in 1814. After his death, the doctor's descendents, tired of the unwarranted burden that the family moniker brought them, lobbied to get the government to formally change the name of the execution device. When the Paris court refused, the children gave up—and changed their name.

France passed a law in the early 1800s that prohibited the use of all baby names except those on a pre-approved list. Although it had not been enforced in years, the last of these statutes was not officially removed until 1993; at that time, the top three banned names were Onassis, Juliet, and Babar.

There are more dogs in Paris—approximately 300,000—than there are children.

80,000

dogs in Paris with private
health insurance

20 TONS

amount of poop dogs leave on the
streets of Paris each day

650

people per year who are hurt so badly
after slipping on dog poop in Paris that
they have to be taken to the hospital
(Broken collar bones are the most frequent injury.)

€ 475

current fine for leaving dog
poop unscooped

The Boar Hound was a dog developed in Germany to hunt large game. When the breed made its way to Paris, French naturalist Georges Louis Leclerc (Comte de Buffon) mistakenly thought that the breed had come from Denmark, so dubbed it the grand *Danois*, or "Great Dane."

French illustrator Francisque Poulbot is well known for his drawings of war orphans in the Montmartre district in 1914. Two of his characters, a girl named Nenette and a boy named Rintintin, inspired a pair of handmade yarn figures that Parisian kids gave to the American servicemen as good luck charms during World War I. When U.S. Corporal Lee Duncan rescued a pair of pups from a bombed-out kennel at the end of the war, he named them after Poulbot's creations, and took them home with him to Los Angeles. Nenette got ill and died shortly thereafter; Rintintin, better known as Rin Tin Tin, became a major movie star, and is credited with saving the fledgling Warner Brothers Studios from bankruptcy.

Every year on the feast day of Saint Francis of Assisi (the patron saint of animals), the Sainte Rita Church in the 15th arrondissement celebrates with a Blessing of the Animals service. Catholics from throughout France fill the pews, in the company of their pigs, goats, sheep, cows, horses, chickens, dogs, cats, hamsters, turtles, rabbits, and goldfish (and that's just in the first row!) that come to receive a blessing. This is a tradition throughout Europe.

Under an arcane Paris law still on the books, it is illegal to name a pig Napoleon.

The song of a nightingale can be heard amid the artifacts and recycled archeological remnants in Georges-Cain Square in the 3rd arrondissement—although it isn't a bird responsible for the soothing sounds, but a sculpture by Erick Samakh, which produces the song when wind blows through the artwork.

There is a school for beekeepers and an apiary that contains two or three hives—housing roughly a million bees—tucked away in the Luxembourg Gardens. In September, the honey is harvested and sold in the park, near the intersection of rue de Guynemer and rue de Vaugiraud.

The bees found within the city of Paris produce up to three times more honey than those living in the country, thanks to more abundant food sources and slightly warmer weather.

Despite having been in business at the same location in the Les Halles district for over 135 years, Aurouze, a pest-control supply store—easily recognizable by the twenty-one perfectly preserved dead rats that hang in the front window—has recently become a major tourist attraction. The owners of the shop lent its name and its nineteenth-century facade (albeit in animated form) to the Oscar-winning film *Ratatouille.*

Although they would be loath to admit it, the best-known (and most expensive) restaurants, food stores, and hotels in Paris all have rat poison sprinkled throughout their basements. The law requires it.

Paris, a city known for its perfume, even has one formulated to freshen up the Metro. Named Madeleine, it is a mix of vanilla and musk. Each month, one and a half tons of the fragrance is added to the cleaning products that are used to scrub and scour the train cars and the stations.

The dramatic height of the glass roofs in most of the Paris railway stations was not simply a design choice, but a necessity. At the time they were built, trains were steam-powered and had the roofs not been elevated, passengers and staff could have suffocated from the toxic fumes.

The dark green cast iron pillars throughout the Gare du Nord train station are hollow. In addition to supporting the station's glass ceiling, they double as drain pipes for the rainwater that falls on the roof.

The Gare d'Orsay, once the grande dame of Paris train stations, fell into disuse and, by 1962, was scheduled to be torn down. In Paris at that same time, filming a movie based on Franz Kafka's *The Trial*, director Orson Welles learned his producers had run short of money and would not be able to fund the next segment of filming in Yugoslavia. So, Welles decided to rent the old station for use as his studio. This unexpected intercession delayed the station's demolition and gave preservationists time to lobby the Ministry of Culture to save the building. Today the old Gare d'Orsay is the Musée d'Orsay, world-renowned for its collection of Impressionist artworks.

Legend has it that French film director Francois Truffaut once picked up a hitchhiker near Paris and started a conversation with him about the movies. When it turned out that the man did not know enough about the subject to converse intelligently with the passionate filmmaker, Truffaut stopped the car and made him get out.

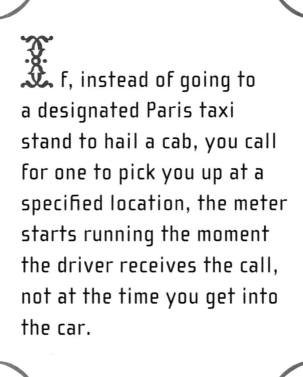

If, instead of going to a designated Paris taxi stand to hail a cab, you call for one to pick you up at a specified location, the meter starts running the moment the driver receives the call, not at the time you get into the car.

Only 2 percent of daily transportation in Paris is by taxi. While approximately 15,000 cabs circulate the city, more than 25,000 people are looking to hail one at any given time.

It is fortunate that it rarely snows in Paris—the city has no snow removal equipment.

There is an atomic bomb shelter—originally built in 1939, still perfectly intact, and big enough to hold seventy-two people—hidden under Tracks 2 and 3 at the Gare de l'Est train station.

PARIS FACTS

There is a Metro station within 500 meters (about one-third of a mile) of every building in Paris.

131 MILES
length of track in the Paris Metro

3,500
cars in the Paris Metro

380
Metro stations

750,000
travelers per day using the Chatelêt-Les Halles, the world's largest subway station

5.6 MPH
speed of the automated sidewalk in the transfer tunnel of the Montparnasse-Bienvenue Metro station

A number of Paris Metro stations were closed at the start of World War II, when some of the transport staff was called into service. Although the decision was made not to re-open most of them after the war, few have gone unused: Arsenal now houses facilities to train electricians and engineers; Saint-Martin has doubled as a homeless shelter; and the idle portion of Porte-des-Lilas (the area behind the public platforms) is leased out to film companies who need to recreate the Paris Metro for TV or movies.

A functioning Metro station was built at Haxo, between Porte-des-Lilas and Pre-Saint-Gervais, but due to last-minute changes in the original plans for the Metro system, it was no longer needed—and so no access to street level was ever constructed.

The Clignancourt line of the Paris Metro makes a marked, but purposeful, swerve to the east as it travels between Saint-Germain-des-Pres and Les Halles. This is because underground trains cause vibrations; hence, if the track had been laid in a straight line between these two stations, the train would have passed directly beneath the Académie Française...and the vibrations would have disturbed the scholars at work there.

The Académie Française—the official moderator on all aspects of the French language—recently banned the term "e-mail," replacing it with *courriel*, which is short for *courier electronique*. This is part of its ongoing effort to stop English words from seeping into the French lexicon.

Étienne de Silhouette, finance minister under Louis XV, earned a nationwide reputation as a parsimonious penny pincher when he attempted to balance the national budget by ordering the melting down of all items made of gold and silver. So synonymous was Silhouette with "cheap" that when shadow portraits—profiles cut from black paper, which could be gotten for a fraction of the cost of a real portrait—became popular, people referred to them as "silhouettes."

After Charles Perrault, a lawyer, lost his post as secretary of the Academy of Inscriptions and Belles-Lettres at the age of sixty-seven, he published a compendium of fairy tales. Included in the book was his revamped version of *Cinderella*, to which Perrault contributed the pumpkin coach and the fairy godmother. He also changed the material of Cinderella's famous slipper from *vair* ("fur") to *verre* ("glass").

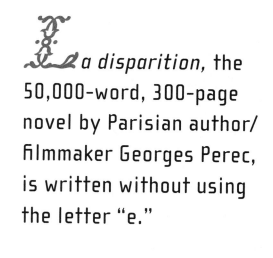

La disparition, the 50,000-word, 300-page novel by Parisian author/filmmaker Georges Perec, is written without using the letter "e."

From his factory in Paris in 1945, French businessman Marcel Bich, satisfied with the success of his disposable ballpoint pen in Europe, decided it was time to take on the international market. Realizing that Americans would incorrectly pronounce its name, he smartly dropped the "h" and simply called his pen Bic.

When Emily Dickinson's sister Lavinia discovered her cache of poems after her death, many of them were written on odd bits and scraps of paper, including prescription blanks, shopping lists, drugstore flyers, and Chocolat Menier wrappers.

By the mid-twentieth century, Chocolat Menier would become one of Paris' premiere chocolatiers, but it was founded in 1816 to manufacture pharmaceuticals. Chocolate was not a company priority; it was merely produced as a medicinal powder or to be used as a coating for bitter-tasting pills.

While Americans usually cut asparagus with a knife and fork, in France, it is one of the few foods that can (and should) be eaten with the hands. The general rule of thumb? Lift a spear by the large end and take bites starting at the tip. Continue doing so until about a quarter of an inch of the stalk remains; that piece should be left uneaten on the plate.

In 1956, Noel Carriou got so mad when his wife made the roast beef too rare that he kicked her out of bed with such force she fell to the floor, broke her neck, and died. After serving a seven-year prison sentence, Carriou was released and subsequently married again. When his second wife overcooked the roast, Carriou stabbed her to death. A Paris jury, perhaps sympathetic to one man's passion for good food, sentenced him to only eight years behind bars.

When dining at someone's home in Paris, etiquette dictates that you arrive about fifteen minutes late for dinner, yet right on time for lunch. Never bring wine; that's tantamount to saying what the host is serving is not good enough. If you opt for flowers, make them low-maintenance, and make sure that they are neither yellow (a symbol of infidelity) or chrysanthemums (synonymous with funerals).

Poubelle, the French word for garbage can, owes its name to Eugene Poubelle, a nineteenth-century Paris official who decreed that landlords must supply each tenant with a covered bin for the purpose of collecting rubbish.

Today, Paris is the only world capital with daily trash collection.

Although commonly thought of as a fashion accessory for the impeccably dressed man, the boutonniere had its beginnings on the Paris streets, where both men and women would put flowers in their button holes to mask the unpleasant smell of garbage that was so prevalent throughout the city.

In the mid-1880's, when ragpickers set up business in Saint-Ouen, near Paris, the clothing they sold was often flea-ridden. As a result, the marketplace became known as Marche aux Puces, the "Flea Market."

Anyone without the connections to finagle a front row seat at Paris Fashion Week can still see the latest haute couture trends—and do it for free. On the seventh floor of the Galeries Lafayette department store, on Fridays from March through December, thirty-minute fashion shows are presented.

Worried that the high-heeled shoes he had designed did not look "finished," Christian Louboutin noticed a woman in his design studio filing and polishing her nails. Inspired, he grabbed the bottle of red nail polish from her and proceeded to color the sole of his latest shoe. The red sole became Louboutin's signature.

The iconic Hermès Birkin bag was inspired by—and named for—actress and '60s cover girl Jane Birkin, after she unwittingly found herself seated next to Hermès CEO Jean-Louis Dumas in 1984 on a flight from Paris to London and, in the course of conversation, described for him the perfect weekend tote.

By the Numbers

$7,500
starting price of a Birkin bag,
not including sales tax
(The cost can easily reach five or six digits,
particularly when the bag is constructed from
exotic animal skins.)

2 YEARS
minimum wait time for a Hermès Birkin bag

250
mulberry moth cocoons needed to generate
the silk woven to make one Hermès scarf

2,500
scarf designs Hermès has produced since 1937

500,000
Brides De Gala scarves sold to date
(Hermès' No. 1 seller)

Only 1 percent of the items bearing the trademark Louis Vuitton monogram are authentic. This is ironic because it was widespread copying of early Vuitton patterns, and the need to prevent counterfeiting, that pushed the family to first design the legendary "LV" monogram canvas in 1896.

In November 2007, Louis Vuitton successfully sued over a Britney Spears video for copyright infringement. In her video for the song "Do Somethin'," Britney drives a pink Hummer with a counterfeit Vuitton "cherry blossom"-monogrammed dashboard. Britney herself was not found liable, but a civil court in Paris ordered music producer Sony BMG to pay $117,600 for damages to Vuitton's image.

The original Louis Vuitton workshop in Asnières, just outside Paris, produces about 450 made-to-order and custom-designed pieces a year. One-offs have included a case for a silver hookah pipe and a carrier outfitted with individual drawers for thirty shirts and thirty ties, plus a special little drawer for cufflinks. However, the most infamous (and decadent) of all orders was The Willy Trunk: a perfectly crafted miniature model made for a businessman—to carry his rubber duck named Willy.

ouis Vuitton raised
eyebrows in the 1940s
when the company set up a
factory and began producing
and selling mementos
(including more than
2,500 busts) that glorified
Philippe Petain, whose Vichy
regime was responsible for
the deportation of almost
76,000 French Jews to Nazi
concentration camps.

Paris' famed five-star Le Meurice hotel served as Nazi headquarters for occupied France during World War II.

Shopping in Paris may be synonymous with boutiques from haute to hip, but the place not to be missed is the unique and eclectic Deyrolle. This 100-year-old taxidermy shop (yes, you read correctly), located in the 7th arrondissement, is a two-story natural history museum except the one-of-a-kind minerals, fossils, insects, butterflies, vintage teaching tools, and amazing stuffed stuff are all on display for sale.

250

bouquinistes (used book sellers)
lining the Seine around Notre-Dame

8 YEARS

current time on waiting list to
become a bouquiniste

$150

rent per year for each bouquiniste

2

bouquinistes selling nothing but
Jules Verne books in the
original bindings

Philosopher and writer Jean-Paul Sartre was the second cousin of doctor, humanitarian, and Nobel Peace Prize winner Albert Schweitzer. Because of the difference in their ages, Sartre always referred to Schweitzer as "Uncle Al."

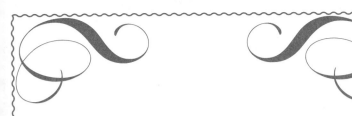

Sartre had an extreme phobia of sea creatures—shellfish in particular—and was terrified of being attacked and dragged underwater.

Poet Gérard de Nerval had a pet lobster that he would take for walks along the streets of Paris—for shock value, if nothing else.

Although he authored ninety-seven works totaling 11,000 pages in the span of twenty years, Honoré de Balzac feared his creative energy could be sapped if he ejaculated during sex. He considered sperm a "cerebral substance," believing that when it was released from the body, thoughts and ideas went with it.

The modest house Balzac brought in the 16th arrondissement in 1840 was specifically chosen because it had two separate entrances— one on rue Raynouard and another leading to rue Berton. The unique setup allowed him to slip out unnoticed through one door, when creditors or unwanted guests showed up at the other.

Both Balzac and Voltaire fueled their literary output by drinking more than fifty—and possibly as many as seventy-two—cups of coffee a day.

While there is a large sarcophagus inside the Pantheon in Paris inscribed with Voltaire's name, the burial site is empty. Before he was interred, the writer's heart and brain were removed; later, a group of his enemies decided that a formal gravesite was not deserved, so they broke in, stole his remains, and dumped them in a garbage heap where they lay undiscovered for more than fifty years.

Marie-Antoinette never said, "Let them eat cake," nor was she cold-hearted and oblivious to her people's suffering. The "let them eat cake" incident has been attributed to a Grenoble princess in 1740. French revolutionaries who hated Antoinette for her Austrian blood and her frivolous ways simply borrowed the story and ascribed it to the queen (who wasn't even born until 1755) in an attempt to damage her reputation. Their plan worked.

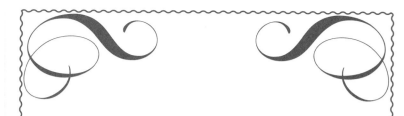

Paris may be the most romantic city in the world, but it was not named for Paris, the beloved of Helen of Troy. Rather, the city took its name from the Parisii, a tribe of Gauls who established a fishing village on the banks of the Seine around 250 B.C.

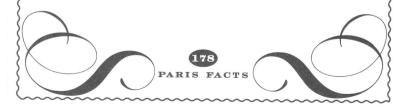

boulevard was originally a military engineering term for the level part of a defensive wall where canons were placed. When the wall that ran through Paris was torn down in the late eighteenth century, the wide civilian promenade that replaced it kept the martial name. That's how the road became known as Grands Boulevard—and how large roadways everywhere eventually came to be known as boulevards.

In 2007, in a move to preserve the Champs-Élysées' reputation as city's most prestigious address, the Paris government passed a law to ban any more global chain stores from setting up shop on the celebrated avenue.

30 MINUTES
average time it takes to walk from one end of the Champs-Elysees to the other

394 FEET
width of Avenue Foch, the widest street in Paris

6 FEET, 7 INCHES
width of rue de Venise, the narrowest street in Paris

3 FEET, 11 INCHES
width of the narrowest house in Paris, located at 39 rue de Chateau-d'Eau

There is a good chance that a home or building in Paris with a vintage address plaque that features larger-than-normal street numbers—such as the one found at 36 rue Saint-Sulpice in the 2nd arrondissement—was once one of the city's 195 brothels. Prostitution was legal until the mid-1940s, and the oversized numbers were a subtle way to help interested parties find what they were looking for.

In the first Harry Potter book, Nicolas Flamel was referred to as the maker of the Philosopher's (or Sorcerer's) Stone and a close friend of Hogwarts' Headmaster Albus Dumbledore. Not only was Flamel a real person—a French bookseller, calligrapher, and alchemist who, legend has it, could turn lead into gold—but his house at 51 rue de Montmorency in the 3rd arrondissement is believed to be the oldest house in Paris.

With its steel framework, glass block walls, and sliding partitions, the Maison de Verre (House of Glass) in the 7th arrondissement is a stunning example of early modern architecture. The owner planned to demolish an existing row house to build the new residence, but the upstairs tenant refused to leave. So, Pierre Chareau, the architect, demolished the bottom three stories of the building, and built the new residence around her.

As Louis XIV's Finance Minister, Nicolas Fouquet made two major errors: First, he built the Vaux le Vicomte, a spectacular estate outside Paris that outshined the king's own manor—and then he had the audacity to invite the king to see it. Furious at having been upstaged, Louis XIV summoned Fouquet's architect, decorator, and gardener, and put them to work creating an even bigger and better home: Versailles. As a final coup, the king saw to it that Fouquet was falsely charged with embezzlement, and had him tossed in jail.

In the early days of Versailles, the outside guards whistled when Louis XIV approached, so the gardeners could have the fountains fully running whenever he arrived at any given spot.

50
fountains in and around Versailles

620
fountain nozzles that send the water upward
in bubbles, blades, tongues, or sprays

147
hydraulic effects "performed" in the
Neptune Basin, where the Nocturnal
Illuminations take place

951,019 GALLONS
amount of water used per hour when all
fountains are in full play

8
fountain technicians employed at Versailles

When standing in the gardens and looking at Versailles, the central part of the palace is not what it seems, because there are no rooms behind the windows on the top floor; those windows mask the structural supports for the ceiling of the Hall of Mirrors.

The grounds at Versailles include a working farm. Through the years, the crops have included wheat, pineapples, and coffee beans.

150
varieties of apple and peach trees in
the vegetable garden at Versailles

48
full-time gardeners employed
at Versailles

700
rooms in Versailles

67
staircases in Versailles

1,250
fireplaces in Versailles

Louis XV requested motorized tables for the dining rooms in the Petit Trianon at Versailles. The idea was that when the family was ready to eat, a table would rise automatically from the kitchens below, fully set. Although the actual furniture was never built, the mechanics are still in place.

During the reign of Louis XIV, a hat and a sword were considered proper attire for gentlemen visiting the Grand Apartment at Versailles; those without could rent them at the front gate. Monks were not allowed inside.

The drilling process that allows uncontaminated water to rise and flow upward without the need for pumping was uncovered by monks in the province of Artois, which is why the wells that work on this principle—including the ones that provide Paris with water—are called artesian.

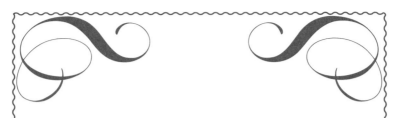

In the twelfth century, monks introduced a racquet into the handball game that they played against monastery walls, and modern tennis was born. The name came later. When French nobility latched onto the sport, their servants took to calling "Tenez!" ("Hold on," or "Take heed"), just before the ball was put into play.

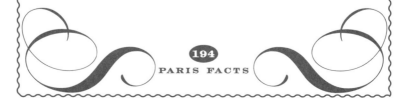

In tennis, the term "love," used to denote that a player has no points, might have evolved from the French word *l'oeuf* meaning "egg," and the egg's similarity in shape to a zero.

Blaise Pascal and Pierre de Fermat, a pair of mathematicians in Paris, came up with the theory of probability after being asked by a gambler friend to figure out a gaming strategy that would enable him to beat the house at a particular dice game.

When songwriter and bandleader Ray Noble wrote the classic song "Paris in the Spring," he had yet to visit the city; his inspiration came from a travel poster that he saw in a London storefront.

DISCLAIMER

All facts, figures, statistics, stories, quotes, and anecdotes found on these pages were checked (and double-checked) and believed to be true (or have some semblance of truth) at the time the book went to press. But things change; stuff happens. So cut me some slack if they're not.

ABOUT THE AUTHOR

David Hoffman is a television writer, a frequent on-camera correspondent, and the author of over a dozen books about popular culture, for which, in recent years, he has been paid to play with toys, challenge untapped cooking skills (with the help of some big-name chefs), and eat and shop his way across the country. He lives in Los Angeles, where he likes to pretend this is hard work.